*Poetry Collection*

# Poetry Collection

### Michael McNeilly

Copyright © 2019 Michael McNeilly

The moral right of the author has been asserted.

Apart from any fair dealing for the purposes of research or private study, or criticism or review, as permitted under the Copyright, Designs and Patents Act 1988, this publication may only be reproduced, stored or transmitted, in any form or by any means, with the prior permission in writing of the publishers, or in the case of reprographic reproduction in accordance with the terms of licences issued by the Copyright Licensing Agency. Enquiries concerning reproduction outside those terms should be sent to the author.

This is a work of fiction. Names, characters, businesses, places, events and incidents are either the products of the author's imagination or used in a fictitious manner. Any resemblance to actual persons, living or dead, or actual events is purely coincidental.

ISBN 978 0993195 419

British Library Cataloguing in Publication Data.
A catalogue record for this book is available from the British Library.

Printed and bound in Great Britain by 4edge Limited
Typeset in 11pt Aldine401 BT by Troubador Publishing Ltd, Leicester, UK

CONTENTS

| | |
|---|---|
| A Tragic Love Story | 1 |
| Jeanne, Comptess de la Motte | 2 |
| Charlemagne | 3 |
| Deirdre and Naoise | 4 |
| The Chameleon | 5 |
| The Wedding Ring | 6 |
| A New Testament Story | 7 |
| Philemon and Baucus | 8 |
| St. Catherine | 9 |
| Hercules and Deianira | 10 |
| Hero and Leander | 11 |
| Pentecost | 12 |
| A Grateful King | 13 |
| Crispin and Crispianus | 14 |
| A Woman with a Tragic End | 15 |
| The Bold Cassandra | 16 |
| A Wicked Woman | 17 |
| The Miracle of Births | 18 |
| Cressida and Troilus | 19 |

| | |
|---|---|
| A Tragic Death | 20 |
| The King's Ruby | 21 |
| Hugh of Lincoln | 22 |
| Hercules and Omphale | 23 |
| The Devil's Messenger | 24 |
| The Bride of the Sea | 25 |
| The Golden Fleece | 26 |
| The Patron Saint of Archers | 27 |
| Tragic Laodamea | 28 |
| Colbronde | 29 |
| Sixteen String Jack | 30 |
| True Christianity | 31 |
| Epimenides | 32 |
| A Wedding Day Prediction | 33 |
| Belphoebe | 34 |
| Tom Hickathrift | 35 |
| True Heroism | 36 |
| Marriage in Haste | 37 |
| Snowing | 38 |
| A Prognostication | 39 |
| St. Keynes Well | 40 |
| Web of Penelope | 41 |
| Rescued | 42 |

# A TRAGIC LOVE STORY

Procris the wife of Cephalus was in distress
She thought that her husband had a mistress
So, she in a very jealous whim
Ran away, thus deserting him
But Cephalus was determined his wife to pursue
Thus demonstrating that to her, he had always been true
While Cephalus was resting under a tree
Procris came upon him quite secretly
Hiding in the bushes, on her husband she was spying
To ascertain, if he was with another woman lying
In those very same bushes, Cephalus heard a sound
Wild beasts in this vicinity did abound
Thinking it was a wild beast which in the bushes did lurk
To kill the wild beast he did not shirk
Hurling his javelin at the bush, as he would have done to his foes
But then… he heard the voice of a woman in her death throes
The heart of poor Cephalus with sorrow did ache
For he killed Procris by mistake!
WIth the very same javelin, he had killed his wife
He employed it now to take his own life

## JEANNE, COMPTESS DE LA MOTTE

Jeanne, Comptesse de la Motte
A very clever theft did plot
Cardinal de Rohan she did persuade
More than one million lives to trade
A diamond necklace for the Queen to buy
But ah! The Countess was so very sly
The diamond necklace she would carry
To the intended recipient Madame de Barry
But Madame de Barry the necklace never received
Thus Cardinal de Rohan himself was deceived
When the jewellers their payment did demand
The Queen disclaimed the matter out of hand
Rohan and Jeanne de la Motte were subsequently arrested
But Rohan stoutly his innocence protested
as a result of the evidence being submitted
After the trial, Rohan was acquitted
The Cardinal, who was even now so reviled
To the Abbey of La Chaise-Dieu was exiled
As for Jeanne the Countess, she came to grief
When she herself was branded a thief
After the Countess had been berated
She was in the Salpetriere incarcerated.

# CHARLEMAGNE

Charlemagne (Charles the Great) was ruler of the Franks
Among the great leaders of the past he certainly ranks
Charlemagne was no less than eight feet tall
In the palace an eight feet long bed they had to install
He was also a man of superhuman strength
And he was to demonstrate this at length
Three horseshoes together in his hand he would bend
So in two he could any wild beast rend
Over western Europe Charlemagne ruled
In matters of the law he was certainly schooled
He was determined to protect Christs body of the Church
So no one would dare his reputation besmirch
His private life with King Henry the VIII we can compare
There is something in common with King Henry he did share
Charlemagne is probably the butt of nursery rhymes
For he was married no fewer than nine times!

## DEIRDRE AND NAOISE

Dierdre was the king's story teller's daughter
King Concholar was one who sought her
At her birth disaster to Ireland was foretold
and this disaster would gradually unfold
Dierdre by King Concholar was reared
But towards the king Dierdre was in no way endeared
She fell in love with Naoise, the eldest of three brothers
Though she may have fallen for many others
Deirdre, Naoise and his brothers all fled
When she and Naoise were to each wed
Then all back to Ireland Concholar enticed
But they oblivious to the fact, that with danger they diced
When Concholar had enticed them back to Ireland again
He made sure that Naoise and his brothers were all slain
But marriage to Deirdre was Concholar denied
She made sure of this by committing suicide.

# THE CHAMELEON

A wonderful creature is the chameleon
Of all living things it is perhaps on in a million
It lives on air – that is according to Pliny
But, I don't know if it's skin is shiny
According to Pliny, but I don't know if it's right
It can change to any colour – except white
It's colour can change from black to that of a proverbial green
    bottle
That is according to the Greek philosopher, Aristotle
It's changing colour symbolises a loyalty that is not steadfast
And it's eyes can look into the future and the past
The chameleon is depicted as Satan in Christianity
Though this view might not be shared by all humanity
In Africa it is not viewed with disdain
Because there it is believed to be the bringer of rain

# THE WEDDING RING

Iartaro, the Basque Cyclops had a talking ring
He was sure that it would good luck bring
He gave it to a girl, whom he wished to wed.
She put the ring in her finger and this is what it said
'You there and I here' the ring kept on repeating
But the ring's behaviour was only self-defeating
In order to rid herself of this ring so fantastic
The girl, beside herself, did something quite drastic.
She cut her finger off, that she'd put the ring upon,
Threw it into a pond – ring and finger both gone
Thus Iartaro's aim to marry this girl had been baulked
By a magic ring which itself only nonsense talked!

# A NEW TESTAMENT STORY

The one hundred and twenty disciple heard the sound of a hurricane
But to them it sounded like a quiet refrain
When each of them sat down tongues like of fire
But they were not alarmed, the chosen tongues were not dire
There then occurred a veritable miracle
When they uttered words, the words were lyrical
Their words in foreign languages were translated
That this was a miracle cannot be overstated
To visitors in Jerusalem, their own languages were audible
These foreigners considered the disciples new found skills to be laudable
However, some observers to the depths of depravity sunk
When they taunted the disciples and said they were drunk
For all that happened that day at Pentecost the holy ghost was the interpreter
This miracle the critics of the new fangled religion would not ignore

## PHILEMON AND BAUCUS

Though Philemon and Baucus were very poor
Travellers they entertained with demur
Their hospitality turned out to be very wise
Jupiter and Mercury visited them in disguise
The grateful Jupiter then did something strange
Their cottage into a temple he did change
The priest and priestess he did them make
Obliging them priestly functions to undertake
Philemon and Baucus then asked Jupiter whether
They might be allowed to die together
This request for them Jupiter granted
After death as trees they were planted
Philemon, when he died, became an oak
To become a linden tree was Baucus yoke
And as if their hearts for each other pined
Both trees branches at their tops intertwined

## ST. CATHERINE

St. Catherine as well as being a saint was also a martyr
Being of noble birth she never had to beg or barter
Of being a christian she made no pretence
In favour of CHristianity she put up a spirited defence
The Emperor ordered her to be placed on a wheel like a chaff cutter
A prayer to Jesus she probably did utter
However Catherines bonds fell off when the wheel began to move
No one can certainly the miracle disprove
Because of this miracle Catherine herself was eventually beheded
This version of martyrdom is folklore embedded.

# HERCULES AND DEIANIRA

Deianira was the wife of Hercules
The facts we know about her are these
Nessus the centaur carried her across the river
He tried to assault her which made her quiver
However, Hercules with a poisoned arrow shot Nessus dead
Thus receiving the girl whom he was to wed
However before Nessus died (who was certainly no eunuch)
He gave Deianira his blood soaked tunic
He told her it would keep Hercules true
Hercules with fidelity it would endue
Deianira gave to Hercules the coast she did acquire
But the poisoned blood caused Hercules to expire

# HERO AND LEANDER

Hero, a priestess of Venus, fell in love with one Leander
Against her loved one no doubt she would hear no slander
Leander who loved her, would cross Hellespoint every night
Leander swam across Hellespoint with all his might
One night when Leander to Hero did not appear
Poor Hero began the worst to fear
When eventually Leanders body was found
It was discovered that poor Leander has drowned
Hero, grief stricken, brought about her life's termination
This she did in the Hellespoint by asphyxiation!

# PENTECOST

Pentecost was also known as the feast of weeks
This term for Pentecost was preferred by the Greeks
The feast of weeks came at the end of the harvest of wheat
A harvest of full and rank stalks eaten by the elite
Pentecost is also linked with the giving of the law
on mount Sinai deliverd by Moses and in great awe
But it is at Pentecost the disciples receive the Holy Ghost
The power he would give them the disciples would toast

# A GRATEFUL KING

King Henry the Second once lost his way
and in a miller's cottage he did stay
Next morning his courtiers tracked down the king
Who the millers praises did merrily sing
The King in gratitude knighted his host
That he was Sir John Cockle was now the millers boast
A great honour for the miller he planned to have done
To a banquet he invited the miller, his wife and son
Over Sherwood Forest the king made Sir John the overseer
With a handsome salary of three hundred pounds a year.

## CRISPIN AND CRISPIANUS

Crispian and Crispianus are the patron saints of shoemakers
Of divine grace both were partakers
These two brothers were born in Rome
But that city was not to be there permanent home
Both emigrated to Sossions in France
Intending the cause of Christianity to advance
They earned their living by making and mending shoes
When they were not preaching the gospel – Good News!
Each was martyred in the year two hundred and eighty six
Those who martyred them did kick against the pricks!

## A WOMAN WITH A TRAGIC END

Dido (Elissa) was daughter of Belus King of Tyre
Her life would most tragically end by fire
Lichaus, her husband was murdered by Pygmalion
The sad thing was that his murder was by no alien
Aeneas who landed on her shores stole Dido's heart
She hoped with Aeneas a new life to start
But her future she discovered was infinitely blighted
Because her love for Aeneas went unrequited
Her revulsion for the King of Lydia she could not hide
So as a last resort in flames, in agony she died.

## THE BOLD CASSANDRA

Cassandra was of Priam and Hercula the daughter
Apollo the god of music, was the one who sought her
Cassandra was renowned for being a prophetess
She was able to tell the future with success
When apollo's advances to her she spurned
Apollo's contempt for her she surely learned
Apollo created in people the predeliction
Not to believe any more her prediction
But Cassandra's predictions still kept coming true
So her reputation as a prophetess certainly grew.

# A WICKED WOMAN

Candaules, King of Lydia
Had a most beautiful wife
He showed her off to Gyges
but this cost the former his life
Because Candaules wife was a woman most treacherous
She probably was also a woman most lecherous
So to murder her husband she did him force
This was her only way to get Gyges, barring a divorce!
When Candaules was dead she became Gyges bride
Though being compliant in her late husbands murder she always denied

# THE MIRACLE OF BIRTHS

Because the Countess of Henneberg was carrying twins
She accused a beggar of committing one of the seven deadly sins
Since the beggars integrity the Countess did smear
He prayed that she would have as many children as days of the year
One would think this to be impossible but alas!
On Good Friday twelve seventy six, this all came to pass
Thus for this miracle of births was this Countess so famed
And either John or Elizabeth were her children so named.

## CRESSIDA AND TROILUS

To be true to each other, Cressida and Troilus vowed
A gift on each other they then endowed
Troilus gave to Cressida a sleeve
But this would later cause him to grieve
Cressida gave to Troilus a glove
To show for him her so-called undying love
There then occurred something strange
In that, an exchange of prisoners was made
Diomed, three Trojan princesses did arrange
In order to receive Cressida in exchange

## A TRAGIC DEATH

If Roman citizenship you did not possess
Being condemned to death you were qualified
That may seem cruel but nevertheless
If you were not a Roman citizen that was how you died.
If crucified you did suffer anguish
The lowest status you now acquired
On the cross your for days did languish
For it often took days before you expired

Pontius Pilate was truly astonished
That the Lord gave up the ghost after nine hours
By that tragic fact Pilate himself was admonished
He may have said: 'this great man over me towers'

## THE KING'S RUBY

Marco Polo stated that the King of Ceylon
Had the largest ruby he'd ever set his eyes upon
The ruby was as long as a span
and it was as this as the arms of a man
Kubla Khan thought it was a great pity
That the king would not give it to him for the price of a city

# HUGH OF LINCOLN

Hugh of Lincoln, a Burgundian was a saint most renowned
In that the first Carthusian house in England he did found
Becoming Bishop of Lincoln as for his life's story there are some clues
In that he was famous for his benevolence towards the Jews
It would be fair to say that amongst the Jews he gained notoriety
by performing for them acts of charity

## HERCULES AND OMPHALE

Hercules became as gentle as a dove
When he with Omphale fell in love
He then led a totally submissive life
He behaved as though he were Omphale's wife
He spent all his time in spinning wool,
Omphale, herself, over him did rule.
Omphale was dressed in Lion's skin
Hercules a female garment was dressed in.

## THE DEVIL'S MESSENGER

There is a legend which is most absurd
That surrounds the American jay bird
It's the devils messenger in the Southern States
Down there , this bird is one of their pet hates!
Where it goes to each Friday no one can tell
But it is believed it carries sticks to the devil in hell!

## THE BRIDE OF THE SEA

The Doge of Venice was somewhat enigmatic
For he used to throw a ring into the Adriatic
This he did each year on Ascension day
To show that the sea over Venice did hold sway
The ring symbolises a wedding for ever to be
For Venice is known as Bride of the Sea.

# THE GOLDEN FLEECE

Jason set sail with the chief heroes of Greece
In an attempt to find the Golden Fleece
After trials his venture was crowned with success
But he was helped by one Medea nevertheless
Out of gratitude he made Medea his bride
He deserted her and then committed suicide.

# THE PATRON SAINT OF ARCHERS

Sebastian of Archers was the patron Saint
He was shot at with arrows feint
But the archers were not very skilled
For it was not by arrows that he was killed
For he was finally beaten to death ·
Remaining serene perhaps till his dying breath.

## TRAGIC LAODAMEA

Laodamea who was Protesilaus' wife
(after Hector had taken her dear husband's life) …
Begged a favour which was truly unique
That she might for three hours with her dead husband speak
This request of hers was eventually allowed ·
But afterwards she was placed in a shroud.

## COLBRONDE

Colbronde was a Danish giant
Upon him, the Danes were so reliant
The story of his demise is so historic
For he was no match for Sir Guy of Warwick
In killing Colbronde, Sir Guy did succeed
Thus England was Danish tribute was freed

## SIXTEEN STRING JACK

Sixteen string Jack alias John Rann
was a rather eccentric highwayman
He wore sixteen tags – eight on each knee
which were clearly visible for all to see
The authorities up against him ganged
and sixteen string Jack was eventually hanged.

# TRUE CHRISTIANITY

Winning a crown of wild olives should be one of your goals
To demonstrate that the Lord Jesus Christ your life controls
To the victors of the Olympic games it came as a surprise
That the crown of wild olives was the only prize

# EPIMENIDES

Epimenides a Greek poet, had the most astonishing of careers
In that he slept in a cave for fifty seven years
When he awoke from his miraculous rest
He discovered that he was of all wisdom possessed

## A WEDDING DAY PREDICTION

A groom should be in dismay
If his bride does not weep on their wedding day
For if his bride does not weep profusely
The bride and groom will be bound in each other only loosely

# BELPHOEBE

Belphoebe oh Belphoebe
Now tell me, who might she be?
She's a character in Spensers Fairie Queene
The sister of Amoret – one so serene!
She's a huntress and goddess to be precise
But unlike her sister, she's as cold as ice!

# TOM HICKATHRIFT

Tom Hickathrift was a labourer and strong man most defiant
In that, armed with an exle-tree and cartwheel, he slew a giant
He received a reward in which he delighted
He was governor of Thanet after he'd been knighted

# TRUE HEROISM

Great is Diana of the Ephesians cried out the followers of the silver smith Demetrius
But why were these silversmiths making all this fuss?
Because Paul was teaching that there was no Gods made with hands
So upon these craftsmen Paul's doctrine was making the heaviest of demands
Statues of Diana the silversmiths did make
To sell thry would not this craft lightly forsake
Demetrius made sure they all understood
That Paul's doctrine would take away their livelihood
If people believed Paul this would their trade undermine
So that eventually they would not be able to sell another shrine
Paul might well have said of all this people there is none stupider
Than Demetrius in believing that Diana's ring fell down from Jupiter

## MARRIAGE IN HASTE

Come in with your damsel and both make your plans
For here you can be married without licence or banns!

# SNOWING

So it's true after all what the weatherman said
I see Hulda is beginning to make her bed

## A PROGNOSTICATION

If you get married in May, you are very plucky
For marriages in May are considered unlucky

## ST. KEYNES WELL

Husband: let me be the first to drink from St.Keynes' well
Or ours will be a marriage made in hell!

## WEB OF PENELOPE

Penelope was a lady oh so proud
For her father-in-law she was making a shroud
But his shroud, she knew, she must never complete
Until her husband again she would meet
For when her husband will return some day
Her unwanted suitors he will slay

# RESCUED

Calainos the moor met the love of his life
He plucked up the courage to ask her to be his wife
To marry him she did reluctantly agree
But only if he brought her the heads of Paladin three
The heads of Ronaldo, Roland and Oliver
The heads of those three you must deliver
Calainos left for Paris where he challenged them to a duel
He knew it would be a contest most cruel
Sir Baldwin the nephew of Roland volunteered to be first
But Calainos the moor poor Baldwin did worse!
The damsels fear of marrying the moor
Baldwins uncle Roland did allay
To avenge his nephews death he himself the moor did slay